WHERE NONE BEFORE HATH STOOD

Also by the Author

The Oresteia of Aeschylus

Open, Not Glass

Jamestown Narratives

Here on a Mission

WHERE NONE BEFORE HATH STOOD

a poem of Jamestown

BY EDWARD WRIGHT HAILE

drawings by Marc Castelli

RoundHouse, Champlain, Virginia

ROUNDHOUSE
P. O. Box 155
Champlain, Virgina 22438
804.443.4813

Printed in Korea

Book design by Diane Landskroener

TABLE OF CONTENTS

WHERE NONE BEFORE HATH STOOD

Let England know our willingness,
  for that our work is good;
We hope to plant a nation
  where none before hath stood.
To glorify the Lord 'tis done …
— RICHARD RICH IN 1610, *News from Virginia*

I showed one of them my sword, and through ignorance he grabbed it by the blade and cut himself.
— CHRISTOPHER COLUMBUS, LOG OCTOBER 12

… we have performed our duties to the uttermost of our powers and have discovered into the country near two hundred miles, and a river navigable for great ships one hundred and fifty miles.
— CHRISTOPHER NEWPORT, LETTER TO LORD SALISBURY,
JULY 29, 1607

One of us must take charge and musket
The council is all a-quirk-bindings
Send us pencils and no more gentle-pens
— WHO WROTE THIS?

DAY ONE

       waters to the west went dry
hill scraps took form and bit the sunset
the seasick demanded their wages and there were plants
      let there be masts in America
the solomon seal proclaimed
          here is a First Day
        take it ashore and be glad godspeed
    and damn the mosquitoes

     and look
the sparrows were anonymous
    the flora were unadam'd the rivers uneven
and sweet turf tumbled from fair banks under deplorable spring

      unsure inshore
captain Christopher Exploit marched us a furlong to say
     nothing here but meadow briar fragrant paths fair and fine tree sameness

at dusk the people like bears on all fours creeping and gazing
        each with a bow in his mouth wounded a bystander in the palm

        back aboard
the box containing the list of the councilors was opened to no gust but hornets
        who quarreled over sites to build cities in Apamatica

          and a holycross at Cape Henry

we assembled the shallop
the captain had us follow swimmers to Kecoughtan
        who drummed us up a merry welcome
      with a wheel of wry-neck morris dancers
     fed us sod chinquapins and much that was dainty as currants
    captain Consort offered the king to double his cornfields
          bring rye oats and barley for girls
        translated trouble his cornfields and barter rye for pearls

in Paspihe
more of the same featuring a long oration was soft-bound by song
                    that called us otassantassu in perfect meter
        the captain thanked them in giftful good sadness
suggested opening up the whole land mending nightful forests with chanticleer towns
                            calling for corn
        and the werowance or king signaled for another hamper of cleanly cakes

        in Rapahanna
king Pipisco's flute notes fell on places for our footsteps
            went up from moorings on melodies through already magnificent corn
                entertained as otassantassu
                    to crouch and share the pissimor in good humanity
        the captain barely caught himself before too much admiration
                all of us dizzy on mouthfuls of holy rustica
asked him if he dreamt of peace orchards temples towns and squares
            the king said the rest he had in avenues
                    if also at break of day when he washed his face and arms
            the river floated clam shells that was peace

in Archer's hope only the birds came down ground to us
        black crimson watchet yellow green murrey and divers
    without art columnar among vines
  too soft for cages too colorful for pies he told us of hard-bouncing river shoals
        such that you may hear them today

only in Apamatica where the hornets thought the very clouds were cities ready to droplet
    did they treat us like Frenchmen
        and shoot brandish oaths backsides and their cobble swords
    such that captain Cutshort said to turn backsides and drop below

to where decked out afresh as admiralcaptain Christopher Viewfort he now spoke
    moored under the trees of the honk cohonk island
        where at the tramp of oars
        the yellow reed plain lifted shimmering black
        lifted its coal-silver skin crumbling into canvasbacks

peacemaking to say
    this is the river this the river isle
    this shall be re-Virginia
        this riverg in the river I mean in this river beginning
    a great nation where none before

crack went the flying squirrel of George Andrews
and under it we fashioned by sweeping a friendly peeping fort
            with wreath walls turned in half-moon

                in Paspihe

and their letters home flourished with homesick courages
    geese plenty and fat we kill them throwing a stick
    the woods are full of deer turkey and a cattle
    fish to burst our net sturgeon you may ride
    sweet thicket scent of this land sassafrasses far out at sea
    raspberries and herbs and fruit and assentamins

but inserted with discourages rewarding the censor
    have continent please send food clothing shelter
    day long pay short sleep deadly
    Indians too soon water but smelly stumped by tree sizes skies buggy and hot
    we enfortress where none before
    hath stood it an entire summer
    help or I curse god

for in England some had dreamt of gold
    awoke dreaming in Virginia flailing like halfsleepers
    in the understorey flipping leaves with sword tip
    planting holly dowels in gum swamp
    the brains of a toad for your inspection
fresh hands to shovel black barrelfuls of sand ilmenite swung aboard

yea the magic wand of sickness would knight sixty
and dog days make a kettle of quarters

      so that ere the times fell in upon him in this year of grace

emdy-ceevy aye-aye and jacobi regis quinto
on company orders to interleave with the naturals
and smoke their tobacco

captain Christopher Rowboat departing from
the fleet of three ship eight mast and an island in fresh leaf parapet
took shallop provision men marines mariners and gentle manjim dandies
went upjames with an eye for cataracts or seas

whereupon know the river of Powhatan
became if Appalatsy was on the South Sea
the straits of king James or else the river ditto out of Quirank or else America
at each oar-stroked petal-parting mote-waking
bow wave on the pupil of the flood tide

the people of the riverbows awoke
shouted all friends and thronged the waterside hands full
their nakedness seeming
in way of the loose vines and brushwood woven

like the blond logs of river wrack
upright men and women coming down swimming river welcomes
      tamed him with helpings
         of pegatucapon pansaromenans and deer
shaking branches to pelt their guests with mulberries
         as they learned the taste of corn

           the kingdom of Weyanoke was full of musselfuls of pearl
in the sand at the isle of turkeys Kindconsort a savage charted our river with his toe
         until we furnished him with paper plume and well atramental

and stitched our course thereafter with his presence and oyster strings
             for many miles
         along this river the famousest of Christians ever found

at Poor Cottage a boy we saw with white skin within reason and blond got away

              an hour above that
a king spread us mats whose women made us cleanly hoecakes

sod twice a venison and gave captain Showboat his rose of a furry crown
  called him himself
and himself the werowance Arrohatteck of Arrohattecko
no sooner did we camp on his mats
    than another werowance the Tanxpowhatan arrived to two tuneful shouts
and we passed the pissimor some of us still squatted some now cross-legged in state
        in a wreath of sweet smoke before dancers
    who moved as at Kecoughtan with the surf surf of feet
    to the thumb of the limp drum
    and the ricochet gourd's hiss kiss

  we poured one bauble bag watched their glances as the light went new
    and ran in tears of cobalt glass to simple bead amazement
and a second spilling penny knives shears pins farthing bells strung toys in gush amply
        and on the pissimor's third solemn-go-round
    captain Import talked of bringing a cargo of inchplate copper
            saladed with blue beads
    mighty chests of hatchets and a copybook with anyone's name in it

translated matassakwintens or copper canoes
beads bored for wheels the color of violets or
seawater thongs of unnamed leaves in autumn white
and he perceiving their consonance gave it avowal

whereupon
the Tanxpowhatan signaled his present remove
giving us Nawirans to guide us to his crestmont home
where he said he had an horizon we could use

thus we reboated departing Arrohatteck's Joy
to ply oars in the upstreaming evening
over the breathless dip-dimpled water and like so many berry hedges
they as before held out to us along green leaning banks
like sweetbells
or some in shooting canoes
bowls and trays of their country victual
of which nicely our new guide Nawirans requited severalhand

such that ten miles seemed to us a merry five

to come abreast of three peopled islets moored against Salisburyside
                    on Popham was a plain of many early acres
of corn beans peas tobacco popcorn pumpkingreens fist watermillions gourds hempgrass
            sweet-scentedly worked through which we marched twelvesome score yards
up to the house of the king of Powhatan
        or the werowance Tanxpowhatan
        or Parahunt the little mamanatowic
            at home on the last mountain below the fall-line
                    and were there any art all
            goodly habitation

                        they came down weaponless to greet us as we rose in arms
and with Nawirans escort us into their pone village being twelve loaf houses
        some whole some without heels all covered with fresh-husked bark
        some great some shanty and along a street of activities dropped
by women who said butts

Castello 7-24-05

and children whose eyes clung like blackberries
three fingers a gape

and he the Tanxpowhatan
made spread the wayanassayas
or bearskins over phragmite matting
for the whole company and the whole interval
between his company and ours
patting the ground in hospitality so
captain In-port wordless with grinning
flanked by the proud and swordly master Wotton
his interpreter of godsword on the right hand
and captain Smith his interpreter of new worlds without end on his left
who clutched a list of pidgins and a flock of idioms

arrived stood and creaked seams in boot leather and broadcloth
going friendly folded flat
feeling white-kneed and thinking

of a foremast stepping on coral
bade his captain clutchword enlarge on the world's great changes

but the werowance Arrohatteck
      here interruptingly seated again beside the Tanxpowhatan
         spoke cheisk chammay wingapo chemuz
     refreshing the formulas of country welcome to say
          scrub my soul but

what all-aboard brings otassantassu in his three-tun kit shallop
        translated longlegged she-terrapin sanded of every beach
     ascending on rappahanna's pulsing tide?
        translated the river's paw and coon slide under the moon's lopside
come ye among us his corn people and pone folk sit feast tell and talk without time
        translated unending as if hungry in handfed waters
for no man should swim in the flood of hospitality but all drown
        translated be fish please and school flash and founder deeper

                                        on which smiling
captain Showforth said on friendship and discovery
                        and had us shiver the bauble bag in gift shimmer
                                in which new and familiar fed hands gave us their wingapo
                and now softly now louder masked in solemnity
        the captain shared enemies showed wounds scorned our common griefs
                at the hands of the bearish Chesapeakes
                                translated oyster eaters
        for all good people are friends and only criminals and scoundrels are not
                                translated the good the bad the indifferent
the faces of the two werowances
obeyed as that of admiralcaptain Truesort brightened and basked them again in smiles
                and rose crossed and draped his cape about the Tanxpowhatan's shoulders
        because they and otassantassu were cheisk chammay or all one

so the Tanxpowhatan came ahead and pinned his old buck's gown to the captain
        pointed at the sun and vowed major general revenge
                the captain fondled the hilt of his dirk as if to present it
                        thought better of company orders

and we passed the pissimor with a wished eye and in good sadness
    each in turn first cheery then low repeating cheisk or all one

      we departed to see the falls
            exchanging hostages
three miles further up in the shallop grounding below steam
      among great craggy stones and main rock
we climbed aprons of gravel
        in pursuit of veins of glistering spangles
    common between content and grief

and as the evening apple flesh went dusk
returned and rode at anchor beside the three islets
    and the smell of young fields hot after dark

Whitsun tide and captain Beaucourt went ashore on the main isle of grand Manchester
    and had us boil salt pork and peas
    sent Kindconsort to invite the werowances to come join in a huckleberry picnic
    or forage ballasted with our cask and shipstore

and they accepted in good heart liver and spleen
    bringing canoes of their own country victual
or sweet sod chinquapins cakes of pegatucapon strawberries parched meat and land turtle
     and a great company all afeather in clay and fierceface matchqueon
    or antimony paint from a mountain three days' march west then north

          and captain Homeport
   as they landed met them familiarly
    helping them in dishes and helping himself to our fare
  made no sign to sit in state but spoke to each of them in passing
    so that every man stood or sat at randomface or apart in a canopy of talk

they told us where metal was got
  we told them where money was made
they told us the length of the river the distance
  over Monacan's country to the many-veined mountains Quirank
we told them the sea could hide the moon
  but the round world could no longer brotherly love

they asked to see proof
   and whether ships were animals and wind
   and if we needed women or priests
the captain told them he was to pay a visit to Monacan before he left the falls
   noted the Tanxpowhatan took strong exception stifled in stiff courtesy

  now our missing by the way two little bags of truck and shot
the captain ventured to complain of it in right fatherly good sternness
  and the king of Arrohatteck signaled for quiet and instantly caused a full refund
  from as many thieves as the sum of bullets trinkets and toys
        including a knife ere missed
so that captain Christopher Suefort gave thanks and
  rewarded the thieves by returning to them what each had stolen
       keeping back the bullets
  warned them chattily such an offense would mean death in England
but made it plain as words he was framing himself to act mercifully
  prompted by fear of the god of heaven
   who was hairtrigger to wrath but long-arc to love forgivers in kind
  the one true almighty and eternal who would remove the devil's foot

the king of Arrohatteck said their god loved them just as well with all his might
      the one called from day to day Ahone and Rawotenend Mannith or Messapos
who set down all things on earth one by one and exhaled souls into select of them
           but they paid no attention to it

instead they worshiped adored pleaded prayers to the mischievous Oki
      because he was a jealous god quick in wrath and brought them all their misfortune
      they paid him tobacco copper children roanoke and suchlike
      whereas today a helping of a hog butchered in Smithfield

but captain Beausort said never mind
        otassantassu and the Powhatan people from this day forth
shall as one current or clay in ocher build a great nation and wear clothes
              and be folded under happy laws
          translated clay for happy lawyers and foiled kings
      he would begin by making the Tanxpowhatan foiled king of Monacan
    who was right pleased from not believing
and Arrohatteck said a nation is built of souls copper slaves and accuracy of law

but asking what will clothe them
the captain with a lookround said
he expected the lord the prophets and the commandments
and Arrohateck saying he had given that shell a shattering of a thought
had found no meat
the captain said mealy thoughts were like headlong flocks of gun-risen birds
at a report of fact
for his own nation was risen to a powerful fact and mighty edifice of law
and the commandments housed in true cathedrals
so the king of Arrohateck asking then why he was here not there
and he answering to englobe England
their words rejoined the streamers and canopy of talk
for interpreters sortied among them like messengers or children

Nawirans spoke to Tanxpowhatan pointing to another cross
we had made and rested among alders freshhewn and long as a keel
in which captain Beaucourt had his name the year and king James featly incised

and the Tanxpowhatan looked at it asquint
turned to the captain as if to speak

but Arrohatteck asked to hear our guns

but the Tanxpowhatan signed to ask about the cross

but the king of Arrohatteck signed pocossaks or pieces asking to hear fire

but the Tanxpowhatan jerked and gestured all talk all over the island to a mighty cease

soot in his look spoke aloof to the captain's interpreter
who held open his list of pidgins
demanded to know if our cross had a proper deployment and a job

captain Beaucourt thoughtful as if hearing counsel
waited one quaff of a cupstein
to catch the drop of his eye at the last reel of the king's patience
answered as if hearing viols

not properly yet but that this figure fulfilled the lost wax of the trinity
  for he knew he could not answer directly
         or amity and alliance in the bars crossed
     with the names of him and the Tanxpowhatan embossed
       translated holy persimmons amorous ripe *ardor* frost

and the murmur of pumpkin friendship went round

        that it was ready to be put aboard
    and set up on a little stony mat
      or islet of grassy tonsure at the mouth of the falls
   the Tanxpowhatan from knowing where jumped up ran to it
     leant it among many hands on his shoulder
       and as his people thronged and joined him to bear it up
    waded with it across to the dolorous riverbank
   carried it up Salisbury's viburnums through a crowd some laughing some jeering
      as we followed in the shallop and landed on the islet awaiting events

they splashed and strode out in the current above us
        and he
    leaving his people now
launched and straddled the cross to ride it through punch and current down to us neatly
           as if he lay on a bed and a mattress
   and as the current eased we rescued him and brought him into harbor
      dug and raised and beset it with boulders and fill as stout as a tree

               as we worked
   he told the captain one saw only trouble if he wished to march us up to Monacan
      where there was no food and the mountains were sharp and the river divided
      they for their part would visit *him* if one waited until fall of the leaf
        either to come with caquassan or war or to see what had been done
   and the captain promised him five hundred men

now once the cross was up it gleamed over the river like fresh bone
      or as a thing descended moving and making beams
      and he asking again what it stood for
on advice of his pastoral right hand the captain answered

that the waters out of Quirank that flowed around it
were hardly the measure of the blessings to flow from it
translated floods of all things great and good

thence parting met him again as we boated down by the islets before Powhatan's Tower
as master Archer would call it
the captain went ashore alone presented him a hatchet
but again finding the falls werowance of zetetic mien
entraptious to captious Nawirans
the captain told him the true nature of the cross brought down salvation
translated man's best friend
which greatly rejoiced him
thus back aboard we gave him two pretty shouts
he and those with him waved goodbye robes in friendship overhead as we thought

and went out at the ebb on the salt-eager current canyoned by trees
to take supper below at Arrohatteck's Joy
only to discover Tanxpowhatan renewed and party once again beside our host

                    atop his stepped banks
they made spread the wayanassayas over reed
            covering the whole space once more as we came up in state and sat
                        the pissimor was lit and passed one circuit in good sadness

when the werowance Arrohatteck spoke up after due quiet and said tense and toneless
                    we hear from Paspihe
                            translated Jamestown
otassantassu is like the steps of a hurricano
            trees down for the count wherever you come ashore
                        translated Englishmen

                                    but the Tanxpowhatan spoke first to ask him
what the harm was in taking nothing by force but squatting on a little waste ground

indeed he then begged us again in the manner of a host rehearsing a matter
                for household benefit and on the captious cupped whisper of Nawirans
                        as we took it
            what the cross stood for and how long and whose was it

saying

scrub my soul but

brother whatzackly is the meaning of ishere cross

translated Jesus

erected yonder by the powhatan?

translated whose waters fall in tiers

stakin out some sort of a imperial claim?

translated to proclaim man's limit?

the captain answering in friendly brusk and borrowtone as if a small matter

said he should first gratify the old wish of kind king Arrohatteck

and by a wave of his frilly lace-puking cuff our untimely Blowforth summoned

werowingapo thunder of drilling ranks

who translated a cheisk chummy volley of gunfire

which frightened their company less to hear

than to see the shot skip in the river and rattle in the trees

followed with another rolling in slow gatling

relaxed at alarm in his opposite

the captain regathered his squat again bade his vocabularian renewed
enlarge on the nature of the reformed Anglo-Greco-Roman special offer
and Marcusaurelius Diogenes and the too-mystic god
though this time after having sneezed on the Schoolmen coughed up Augustine
to wit

a man is a problem
translated the groping intermediary
word list crinkling at the ready nervous

a formed man
was
let me say a man
was is that is
a man

maynesk? maynesk?

—palisadoed? walled? impaled? staked? fort-mounded?
wattled? wattled! daubed sticks!—*temaahkwew omaynesk neppi!*

a man is like a dammed beaverpond

      the dam represents his work and his education
      gathering his life force for civil and cultural use
      but that if the dam broke and the barrier gave way
      ancient slimy channels would reemerge
      and he would resort unchecked to his former unformed nature
      giving way to the erratic erotic wild covetous rhythmic
      in short savage side

Beausort on cue sweeping his cufflace puffily round at the open-dark woods
      and continentally leading willynilly fluffily
          all eyes in sick light to the bleary west
over the bent buffalo backs of askwewak hilling the fallingaway earlyyoung corn terraces
      or pocatawes rolling below the Joy and across opposite
               sparked with spring floral in Salisbury ascent
and to his vessel in the black shallop-shallow river
      and its pallid gums all a-teeth with canoes

we are the dammed
and bring you good tidings of great joy

now the Tanxpowhatan heard all this as one mouthful
    and the smile never left his cheek or invaded his eye and his ear
                                                never sleepwalked
        albeit Arrohatteck smiled and shivered and looked eveningwards
                but he the Tanxpowhatan could believe it
the beaver was yes an acceptable hush-roar philosopher and pedant of impoundments
            as architect and pencilmaker of solidity in ooze
        and had a tail like all the man-kin but man

            if only one could find a man or a woman with a tail

but had a knack and a willingness and agility
        a man had only in battle
and produced ponds upwards in his generations
        working from the water's branch to the water's confession

gauges the depth of talk as time to crack new marrow
in re the late business of the Honk Cohonk island

in Paspihe
word came already smelt of feces and oldcamp
with
I cannot wait to reward a true friend
I cannot wait to acknowledge a great people
my love and wealth do not wait to change before
the bringers of wealth and love

signals and straightway two stout fellows with great hide bundles approach the midst
of the stately parties and the pissimor halts down the circle of kings
and the Tanxpowhatan at a sign has them
fling laces and roll out towards us as if in attack and assault
pelts of shining beaver creeping and rolling in slant highlight
and buckskin bear otter fox mink and rats brown and forest silver
and sets among them baskets of smoky bored pearl or their corn and sundry
besides a great throw of turkey robes

                                              woven to a kingly fathom
                                        to wit
all going in ox and commodious tandem by weight of change
                        pelts or robes or baskets
                        or baskets pelts and robes
                        or robes in baskets pelts in robes
for pocossaks
                    dockside up
                                    and gunpowder ready for planting

observes a shudder glance nod to the side wag the front rank
            he gauges will make the great mamanatowic at Werowocomoco
                                        scowl in approval
                leaving his guests to breathe and devour all they beheld breathless

                            the captain said we had none to spare
                we gave hatchets and bells and suchlike for pelts and baskets
            then two then three then more to get one pelt much moused
                one weary corn basket pushed much false

one robe for the captain to admire and keep
and so with his liberality spoiling the trade
caused a parade in line of basket bearers
the which
seeing the trade rush
put down their least punnets
and blotted into a push of prong-arm beggars
we quickly ran out of favorite looking glasses
to live in a fog of hawk's bells

the Tanxpowhatan now claps his hands with a clicking of bracelet teeth and files depart
as if eager to hasten to the role
of host over the haunch and the hoecake
right edgy with his waiting dancers losing charge on two feet
all the same deeming oneself etiquette-bound
to reply in state
signed for Arrohatteck to reopen with
wingapo captain New Fort wingapo
child of old Harwich-by-Stour

seadog of the Spanish main
and werowance of three mangaquintens and a shallop
already this week werowance of Honk Cohonk

may we meet like kisses
and part in crescents of friendship down all days

                    but sage Arrohatteck unsure of the dance note
             questions the beaver totem and besides

           goes on with
behold yonder flotilla of young stars
     the seven brights plus a nose and four padding feet
well we call it the great bear
     or mangowayan, ursa major, ἡ ἄρκτος ἡ μεγάλη, Kallisto's mother

but now when a little boy tells the world he's born
     he has come straight down from there
     and so he is soft and fair and foolish with universal devotion

translated controversial emotion
truth is he must toughen up faster than the elements scare him
translated elegance prepare him
or he will if he holds the cord and goes not back in the egg
turn out a pathetic womanless pale creature
translated squawkless male preacher

now passing him the pissimor the Tanxpowhatan
calm in smoke exhales picks up with
but sir

shoot sprint fish stake waters fight and dice
naked but for his pride and the airborne lance honor

thieve yea learning to with snapcourage and terrapin discernment

mankill in the service of straight strength and the true eye

terrify his enemies translated enema pennies
and confound them in the midst of their battle dance

friendly the animals that must slow down to feed us

hate the small repetitious womanly spidery-thin finger quotidian
      bending the manly from the sun-stolen summit
           into the pound pent indoors shutup
      where he watches motes soup across the light
                translated clothed to the wrists
      but fool fake feign bluff laughdart
out of reach like the moon in ripples
                translated fart slippers for the lord in detail
        yessir
        virtue is neither the bellow or smith nor coward or hero
      but always the highscore in the rite of man to man
              translated the rights of man

thus did they summon speech

thus did they preach to the queryfrown
     forehead to forecastle into the swimming night

to the relief of Tanxpowhatan
     silence fullstop had stayed over New Fort on joy
and to the relief of the dogger of seas
     pause came over Tanxpowhatan on light
and he went conciliarly dumb on man
        thinking
        bloodcunning and no philosopher
    we'll see who wins this caterwaul
    stake him nothing and take all

whereas New Fort
        blithe both-hearted giftish and no philosopher
        bethinking him
   I have known many lands and a good many men

he's a fine sort of half-naked savage I ken
precisely the kind to flatter and work

following his eye
     shall I give him my dirk?

did and made shake the bauble bag and poured new troves
     of pins prickneedles quill bonnets
          blue beads buttons corbelled combs rings jimcracks
       besides on blithe bonny impulse soldering thoughts
to say

       have a drink old sire

and the Tanxpowhatan squared his jaw and
     hah
     what was *that?*
     'tis p'isonin' *my* tooth

for any other drink tonight
truth!—
yit's in my head now
like dye or paint throughout it
another swig and I won't do without it
whereupon to his surprise his poplar toppled
      sick and kicking retching

and bellowed in formulas and ancestral nicknames
     and his quiyoccosus or holy dons went all a-fakery mummer
          in unconstrued despair from
     daring use only the sacred secret tongue
          fair tomocomo instead of square uttamatomakkin
     glaring pleas one to another in prayer stoop
          wagging medicine knuckles and tobacco sachets
            whickering in what-whats

but Newfort after the due interval
      helps his fine new Irish friend on his feet
          and walks him nicely
and the Tanxpowhatan drew air and grinned
        and drank water with oafish splash
claimed he was healed by the greatest power on earth
           after the power of Guinness's

but poor king Arrohatteck so dead at his leaden rest and crossing earth orbit lumpily
         was borne away into the night like a yule log

and thereupon clickjingle the dancers came forth
prepped on the theme of peace hatchets and copper
      and at long last made the wheel with the surf-surf of feet
      and the thumb-thumb of the limp drum
      and the sweet school of the flute pool
      and the ricochet gourd's hiss kiss
      and three girls smooth of flank formed the axle hub

and the wry-neck wheel dancers revolved to the axle and the axle sped and sped
and the wheel fled like a bouncing rim faster and faster
down the watercourse over the mounds and stumps and log jams
and tarried swanlike in the grass puddle
beside the mounds and stumps and log jams
and the dam uttered and the waters formed file and went forth as one word

and the patch of darkness hearing it went and pulled the world pendulous from its pocket

in aftertime they tell us
      the people of the country like ants down a log
came all day long and tomorrow
      the halt freak lame and devlishpoorly
to be themselves healed by

      The Great Captain of the Dammed

who verily at the end of his patient purse and of his wallet of diplomacy at bottom
paused only for an agricultural demonstation by the Joy
        and saw Arrohatteck recovering with the dew
           sprint down a thief
    went now like the mallard
      or better the billiard of a prince's progress bank to bank
     at Mulberry Shade Kind Woman's Care Queen Appamatuck's Bower
      Pamunkey's Palace Careless Point Weanock

      as rumor argued in a shell
       widened in a trumpet's bell
  hamlets emptied like blackbirds in treetop awhirr
      Nawirans departed Kindconsort
        gone with the isle of turkeys
    all too late affirming our heating anxieties
   we unbrailed the sprit and filled the sail to buttocks before a fair wind
hastening below to the fort and fleet that had opened the fist of attackers

the day before and driven them off in fingers
        thank heaven and the steady arms of the ready gentlemen

thus seeing their courage begun and their braveries well concluded
        to his satisfaction
        all dice cast to his continent's content
in good order good grief and good sadness
        admiralcaptain Christopher Re-port took leave took ship and farewell
        the two
and twentieth of June
        arriving in the sound of Plymouth on the nine and twentieth
        day of July
        year of Our Lord instant

DAY TWO

now in the years that wallowed in the months that followed
     when the wise grew foolish and the cunning could mince paces
          the fort took angles and
               rotted and rose
               rotted and rose
               rotted and rose

now a maidenly noble hunter doesn't know the difference between god and land
     and land and hell
it's all buttercups drowned furrows and devilswalkingsticks to him
     unless the sun's left in the wheelbarrow of the forest

but tacks at the inference of the animals that sovereignly do know

meanwhile tobacco seed tells your sweatbrow anyway and he
     the Anglo-islander

takes after it boyish each time
        as it girlish takes him each and every time straight
into the Indio-continental's best sweatface ponecorn beans squash millions leaf tobacco

            Opichapam Kekataw and Opecancanu
    dwellers where Pamunkey's ebb and flow marry and single
brothers and heirs of the great mamanatowic at Orapax
        early on asking each other in council
    if the gillyflowers had run out of graves at home
           translate otassantassu
     in time changed their tune to what's an ocean good for
it's a bloody rezone lifting of quarantine
    make this place New-England over my dead body

     O arrow carvers

    humanity itself waits for you to find fight
all-ailing humanity gathers whales on Uttamussak

there on the cliffs the slow Youghtanund shoulders crumbling
is even now the loafhouse choir in the dry dead
and quiyoccosu's daydragging litany and prose to the cast and the rattle
do you hear it?

you know you hear it

if the salt sea did not stop him with thunder
will the land stop him with may apples and springtime?
otassantassu
in his own figure is not Paspihe the bit and Tsenacomaca the horse?
and you will have nothing left his grasp is not under
his guns are mounted and oversee our rivers
his spirits choke the sky
if the woods leave he was the moth
for you see him coming already in the smoky twills from a hundred hunter's glades
bewildering the cardinal points

the ax and crash of his peace repeat the spit fire of his war
you that fair the shaft and true the quill binding
the breezes still
stilling to receive your fletcher's poorwill

yours O arrow smoothers
who else?

the sapling fattens around the tomahawk
bushwhacker arrows make ladders hang shadows in the upright stockade
they should be *men*
cobblestones at low tide beside the waving green flensing reed
ache in sunlight to set a sword and arm your belt
yours *yours*
all days have died leaving the day of *paint*

take off your moccasins take off your matchcoat your turkey mantle
give them to women and
put it on
O arrow-carvers!

we thought they were castaways at once we thought they came as bargain traders
we thought they needed an enclave in the piny bank

we thought they were theologians and bride seekers
thought even a child could engross every ancient law

we thought they smelled of refugees woebegone in provisions

thought they would through tobacco take the first and second hints and needless the third
decamp with their refuse

well *they are thieves they are locusts they are murder smoke and contagion*

and they came out of Pamunkey Mattaponi Nomini
Opiscatumek Warraskoyack Appomattuck and brother Chickahominy
down from grand Chowanoke to great Weyanoke
up from Nansamund Youghtanund Kecoughtund
emptying Menascosic Maracossic Capahosic
Kupkipcock Pawcocomocac Amacauncock Muttamassinsock
in waves out of Nantaughtacund Menapucund Moraughtacund
Paspihe Tappahannock Ocahannock Quiyocohannock

behold how the lice crawl into the bear robe
we shall snatch up the bear robe
string it up from the matted council ground
yea take it and beat it over the fire and the coals

and raise the sound of the surf-surf of feet
the thumb-thumb of the limp drum
the whippoor pool of the flute school
the ricochet gourd's hiss kiss

and the precious blood of christopher fell
that day where rain drooled
the obnoxious odor of burnt offering
snubbed upward
war displayed its privates and spread its buttock brigades
bows sent their sparrow woe aswirl and swan gifts raining
inter-arbor and rising over muddy eyes
squish went the ground ruddy
arrowhead found marrowbed
and flint dint

DAY THREE

the English soul
      ever troubled by its ability to survive justice
defined the grand old enemy and exchequer of impulse
          as a bill of rights
              the fatherless house of mansions at half a score
                  craving no pardon suffering no solomons seal
        the motherless decree with no sister in the fates
    the whipscorn bugger of straight strength and the true eye

for no Indian but an Englishman
      banged the lion's paw right where it first came ashore
at Kiskiack at midnight in a smarting gale prow-burier calling for a blizzard-dizzy
downhelm
      where captain Ian Pounder was pleased to tell a story
          to shush the hostiles and force em into serving cold pudding
     and fill the rites of hospitality among selvage wages

and Werowocomoco yet to come waited
on all branches dripping
with the fresh hung hairfruit of Piankatank

the lion's paw flung out at the new cheek of the lincolngreen world
the lion with heartiest impulse donned an antler coronet
and in the meadows
bloodroot grew beside englishmansfoot

I dub them the sour grapes of silver realization
incorrigible unsalvageables of the land that fools gold
observing another Arrohattecko run a stocking through his stockade
turn and flex a fisted bicep fishlike like a flick tail
and into the far and velvet impenetrable slip

whom we are expected to mint as copper sovereigns and antimony angels

fell to humming in fury over the drought-cracked

painsmaking yawn of a bear mouth's insular hunger
or so Sir Thopas O'Mally midday relaxing the lash to miss his company frumpery and
surveys a new marsh bleed froggy silt ways along his ten-mile log rows to declare
they will not work
take the next one you catch
and try it
give him one wear of pants
a napkin between sermons
no rest
an handful of daily Indian's corn
comb a brass whistle and a submarine
promise of a pair of dice hereafter
and let us see if it gets
another corporal for the cornhill
who wraps a soul for baptism

but Opitchapam as Itoyatin wailed in prayer stanzas
and pentameters of council in the thicket dales as Sasawpen

marshaling his own squadron of bitter ends and unintendeds to say
when our sons return home frisked
and come in from the roaring-chimney college of the Aeneid
writing and reading drinking and rhyming
graduates of Bermudus and William
matriculates of Henricus and Fairy
white as nothing well overhead
spiced with peppered pages from queer-angled sexes
singing six emperors all tyrants
they will no more hunt pray dipfish learnland or even pock by the cornhill
but mutter Virgil rubbing palms smooth as a cobble
and believe the Juvenal smirk whickering whiskey
practice Ovid and the female superior
quoting a horse of the black book a-purpose to
love thy devil-impersonators

at least the young otassantassu still come to us
for brave dress says Kekataugh

the singing hoe-bringing girls
what dancers and courtship mockingbirds they become
and the boys disrobing for tattoos
who want to be hairless
with a cash-and-carry crossbow or a favorite snaphance with storm-green
flint or French in freshet yellow
eyeing the sand seeds of gunpowder
for they shall inherit the earth

until nobody could tell the difference and tell the truth

DAY FOUR

now when the little wanton
        or tomboy svelte
          came to the fort and turned shameless cartwheels in the lanes
            with the best of the hoyboys
they learned she was Amonute
        so she wore clothes and changed her name to Matoaka

and when they heard of that
          she called herself hairdown the bride of Kocowum
        but when the Massawomeck killed him
            or took him off as we thought
she became the doneup wife of master John Rolfe christened
           Rebecca
earning lady Rebecca in England
          only to begin there sitting still to
            princess Virginia

but at the last at Christ's offer in Gravesend
  they drew her little Thames Thomas to her deathbed
and she said to him
  I was always Pocahontas

 and dreamed the wild comic water
   in little big whirlupsmart
  poked under us for occlusion
    grand to pinch abcess fortune injured
     and cold sniffsnuff hidebound
    plumbs a cavernous gravamen

THE END

cohonk, goose

re-Virginia, reestablished after the failure of Roanoke *circa* 1590

i.e., Union Jack crosses of saints George and Andrew

pegatucapon pansaromenans, hoecakes & succotash

Powhatan, a village below the falls of the James River

powhatan, white water

werowance, king, chief

tanx, little, lesser

pissimor, peace pipe

mamanatowic, paramount chief

caquassan, stoneware

askwewak, women

cheisk chammay wingapo chemuze, see Archer's Relation, roughly "all friends howdy one and all"

werowingapo, big howdy (ironical)

cheisk chummy, all friends (ironical)

pokatawes, corn

pocossaks, firearms

wingapo, greetings

mangaquinten, ship

Tsenacomaca, Virginia

englishmansfoot, plantain

Angels are gold coins.

Indians at first believed gunpowder could be obtained by planting & propagation.